SYSTEMATIC THEOLOGY FOR TEENS

OLIVIA ARK

CONTENTS

INTRODUCTION

What This Book Is About

Christianity is more than rules, traditions, or moral advice. As Christians, we understand our faith to be grounded in truth about God, the world, and human life, and those truths shape how we live.

We believe that God exists, that He created the world with purpose, that human beings were made with meaning and value, and that something has gone wrong in creation. We also believe that God has acted to restore what was broken.

This book is about understanding those beliefs more clearly.

Systematic theology is simply a way of organizing what we believe so it can be understood clearly and consistently. Rather than jumping randomly between verses or ideas, it asks clear questions and explains how the Bible answers them.

Each week in this book focuses on one core question of the Christian faith. Not what we are called to do first. Not how we are meant to behave. But what we believe to be true about God, the world, and human life.

What This Book Is Not

This book is not a sermon.

It is not a rulebook.

It is not meant to replace Scripture or the life of the Church.

You are not expected to have all the answers. Growth in understanding takes time, and questions are a natural part of learning. This book is not about performing faith or saying the "right" things.

It is a clear and faithful explanation of Christian belief, written to help understanding grow steadily and confidently.

How This Book Is Organized

The 52 weeks in this book follow a clear progression.

It begins with foundational questions about God, reality, and meaning. From there, it moves through what Christianity teaches about human beings, sin, Jesus, salvation, and what comes next. Each week builds on what came before it.

You do not need to jump around or add extra material. Reading one week at a time is enough. The structure is already there.

How to Use This Book

This book is designed to take about **10 minutes a week**.

Each week includes:

- One main question
- A clear explanation of how Christianity answers it
- A short passage from the King James Bible
- A few prompts to think about

You can read one week at a time. You can read it alone or with others. You can think through the questions quietly or talk about them out loud. There is no required pace beyond one topic per week.

The goal is understanding, not speed.

PART I
WHAT CHRISTIANITY IS

WEEK 1 - WHAT IS CHRISTIANITY ACTUALLY ABOUT?

The Big Question

Is Christianity mainly about rules, traditions, and being a good person, or is it actually making claims about how reality works?

A lot of people hear "Christianity" and think of behaviors, church, or moral advice. But before Christianity talks about what people should do, it claims something about what is true.

The Christian Answer

Christianity is not primarily a set of rules for living. It is a claim about reality.

At its core, Christianity says that the world did not happen by accident. It says there is a real God who exists, who created everything, and who is involved with what he made. Before Christianity tells anyone how to live, it says something about who God is and what kind of world this is.

That is why beliefs matter so much in Christianity. If God is real, then life has meaning beyond personal preference. If God created the world, then the world has a purpose that was not invented by humans. Christianity begins with truth claims, not self help advice.

Christianity also claims that humans are not just random beings trying to survive. It says people were created intentionally, with value, and with responsibility. According to Christianity, the problem in the world is not just bad systems or bad habits. Something deeper is wrong, and it affects everyone.

Because of this, Christianity does not start by saying "try harder" or "be better." It starts by explaining what is true about God, the world, and human beings. Only after that does it talk about how life should be lived.

This is why Christianity is called a faith. Not because it ignores thinking, but because it trusts that what God says about reality is true, even when it challenges how people normally see the world.

What the Bible Says (KJV)

Genesis 1:1

"In the beginning God created the heaven and the earth."

John 1:1–3

"In the beginning was the Word, and the Word was with God, and the Word was God.

The same was in the beginning with God.

All things were made by him; and without him was not any thing made that was made."

These verses show that Christianity begins with a claim about origins. God exists, and everything else comes from him. The Bible does not start with rules. It starts with reality.

Think It Through

- Is Christianity describing what's true about the world, or just telling people how to act?
- If Christianity is true, how would that change the way someone thinks about meaning and purpose?
- Why do you think Christianity starts with God instead of rules?

WEEK 2 - WHERE DOES CHRISTIAN BELIEF COME FROM?

The Big Question

Who decided what Christians believe? Did these ideas just develop over time, or do they come from somewhere specific?

People often assume Christian beliefs were made up by churches, leaders, or traditions. Others think they are just ancient opinions that survived. Christianity, however, makes a clear claim about the source of its beliefs.

The Christian Answer

Christian beliefs are not meant to be personal opinions or changing ideas. Christianity says its core beliefs come from God and are known through Scripture.

Christians believe that the Bible is not simply a collection of human thoughts about God. It is understood as God revealing truth about himself, the world, and human beings. This is why Christian beliefs are treated as something received, not invented.

That does not mean Christians ignore history or thinking. Over time, believers have studied Scripture carefully, discussed it, and organized its teachings. This process helped clarify what Christianity teaches and what it does not. But the source itself did not change. The beliefs were not voted into existence.

Because of this, Christianity does not treat beliefs as flexible depending on culture or preference. Christians believe truth exists whether people agree with it or not. Scripture acts as the standard that beliefs are measured against, not something beliefs are built around afterward.

This is also why Christianity is often described as a revealed faith. It claims that humans did not figure God out on their own. Instead, God made himself known, and those teachings were written down so they could be preserved and shared.

What the Bible Says (KJV)

2 Timothy 3:16

"All scripture is given by inspiration of God, and is profitable for doctrine, for reproof, for correction, for instruction in righteousness."

Luke 1:1–4

"Forasmuch as many have taken in hand to set forth in order a declaration of those things which are most surely believed among us,

Even as they delivered them unto us, which from the beginning were eyewitnesses, and ministers of the word;

It seemed good to me also, having had perfect understanding of all things from the very first, to write unto thee in order, most excellent Theophilus,

That thou mightest know the certainty of those things, wherein thou hast been instructed."

These passages show that Christian beliefs are grounded in recorded testimony and understood as coming from God, not personal imagination.

Think It Through

- Why does it matter whether beliefs are discovered or invented?
- What difference does it make if Scripture is treated as a source instead of a suggestion?
- How might this affect the way Christians handle disagreement?

WEEK 3 - WHY ARE CHRISTIAN BELIEFS ORGANIZED?

The Big Question

If Christianity is based on the Bible, why do Christians organize their beliefs into topics and systems instead of just reading the stories?

Some people think organizing beliefs makes faith cold or complicated. They assume that breaking things into categories takes away from meaning. Christianity, however, sees organization as a way to understand what it already believes more clearly.

The Christian Answer

Christian beliefs are organized because they are connected to each other.

Christianity does not see its beliefs as separate ideas that can be mixed and matched. What Christians believe about God affects what they believe about humans. What they believe about sin affects what they believe about salvation. If one belief changes, others are affected as well.

Organizing beliefs helps Christians avoid confusion and contradiction. It makes sure ideas fit together instead of pulling in different directions. This is what systematic theology tries to do. It does not add new beliefs. It organizes what the Bible teaches so it can be understood as a whole.

This organization also helps Christians explain their faith clearly. Instead of giving scattered answers, they can explain how different beliefs connect. It allows Christianity to be taught, discussed, and passed on without losing its meaning.

Most importantly, organizing beliefs does not replace the Bible. It depends on it. The system exists to serve Scripture, not to compete with it.

What the Bible Says (KJV)

Matthew 22:37–40

"Jesus said unto him, Thou shalt love the Lord thy God with all thy heart, and with all thy soul, and with all thy mind.

This is the first and great commandment.

And the second is like unto it, Thou shalt love thy neighbour as thyself.

On these two commandments hang all the law and the prophets."

Acts 17:11

"These were more noble than those in Thessalonica, in that they received the word with all readiness of mind, and searched the scriptures daily, whether those things were so."

These verses show that Christian teaching is meant to be understood as connected and examined carefully, not treated as random or disconnected ideas.

Think It Through

- Why might unconnected beliefs lead to confusion or contradiction?
- How does organizing ideas help people understand something complex?
- What is the difference between organizing beliefs and inventing new ones?

WEEK 4 - WHAT ROLE DOES THE BIBLE PLAY?

The Big Question

Is the Bible mainly a rulebook, a collection of stories, or something else entirely?

People often reduce the Bible to one thing. Some treat it only as moral advice. Others see it as inspirational stories. Christianity claims the Bible plays a much bigger role than either of those ideas.

The Christian Answer

Christianity teaches that the Bible is God's way of revealing truth about himself and the world.

The Bible is not just a list of commands, and it is not only history or poetry. It is understood as God speaking through human writers to make his will and character known. Because of this, Christians treat the Bible as authoritative, not just helpful.

This does not mean every part of the Bible functions the same way. Some sections tell history. Others use poetry, letters, or teaching. But together, they form a unified message about who God is, who humans are, and what God is doing in the world.

The Bible also acts as a reference point. When Christians talk about beliefs, questions, or disagreements, Scripture is meant to be the standard used to test ideas. Beliefs are not shaped first and then justified later. Instead, beliefs are expected to come from what the Bible teaches.

This is why Christianity depends so strongly on Scripture. Without it, beliefs would drift based on opinion, culture, or personal preference. With it, Christianity claims to stay connected to what God has actually revealed.

What the Bible Says (KJV)

Psalm 119:105

"Thy word is a lamp unto my feet, and a light unto my path."

Hebrews 4:12

"For the word of God is quick, and powerful, and sharper than any twoedged sword, piercing even to the dividing asunder of soul and spirit, and of the joints and marrow, and is a discerner of the thoughts and intents of the heart."

These verses describe Scripture as something active and guiding, not passive or optional.

Think It Through

- Why do you think people often reduce the Bible to rules or stories?
- What difference does it make if the Bible is treated as authoritative rather than optional?
- How might beliefs change if Scripture is no longer the reference point?

WEEK 5 - WHAT DO CHRISTIANS AGREE AND DISAGREE ON?

The Big Question

If Christianity is based on the Bible, why are there so many different churches and denominations?

People often assume disagreement means confusion or failure. When they see different Christian groups, they wonder whether Christianity can really be clear if believers do not always agree on everything.

The Christian Answer

Christianity teaches that not all beliefs carry the same weight.

Christians distinguish between core beliefs and secondary beliefs. Core beliefs are the teachings that define Christianity itself, such as who God is, who Jesus is, and what salvation means. These are the beliefs Christians across history and cultures have shared.

Secondary beliefs involve how those core beliefs are practiced or understood in specific situations. These differences often relate to traditions, leadership styles, or interpretations of less central passages of Scripture. While they matter, they do not redefine Christianity.

Disagreements happen because Christians are human and limited. Understanding Scripture takes effort, humility, and time. Christianity does not claim that believers always agree perfectly. It claims that truth exists and that Christians are responsible for seeking it carefully.

Because of this, disagreement does not automatically mean Christianity is unclear. It often reflects the difference between what defines the faith and what allows room for discussion.

What the Bible Says (KJV)

Ephesians 4:4–6

"There is one body, and one Spirit, even as ye are called in one hope of your calling;

One Lord, one faith, one baptism,

One God and Father of all, who is above all, and through all, and in you all."

Romans 14:1

"Him that is weak in the faith receive ye, but not to doubtful disputations."

These verses show both unity in core beliefs and patience where differences exist.

Think It Through

- Why might it be important to know which beliefs are core and which are secondary?
- How can disagreement exist without destroying unity?
- What problems can happen if all beliefs are treated as equally important?

PART II
GOD

WEEK 6 - WHAT DO CHRISTIANS MEAN BY GOD?

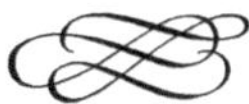

The Big Question

When Christians talk about God, what do they actually mean? Are they talking about an idea, a force, or a real being?

People use the word "God" in many different ways. Some mean a vague higher power. Others mean whatever gives life meaning. Christianity uses the word very specifically.

The Christian Answer

Christianity teaches that God is a real, personal being who exists independently of the world.

God is not part of creation, and he is not dependent on it. Christianity says God existed before anything else and caused everything else to exist. This means God is not limited by time, space, or matter in the way created things are.

At the same time, God is not distant or impersonal. Christianity teaches that God knows, wills, and acts. He is not an abstract force. He is described as speaking, choosing, and relating. This is why Christians talk about knowing God, not just believing ideas about him.

Christianity also teaches that God is the source of all reality. Everything that exists depends on him, but he does not depend on anything.

This makes God different from every created thing. He is not the biggest thing in the universe. He is the reason the universe exists at all.

Because of this, Christianity does not define God by comparing him to human beings or natural forces. Instead, it says God defines everything else.

What the Bible Says (KJV)

Exodus 3:14

"And God said unto Moses, I AM THAT I AM: and he said, Thus shalt thou say unto the children of Israel, I AM hath sent me unto you."

Psalm 90:2

"Before the mountains were brought forth, or ever thou hadst formed the earth and the world, even from everlasting to everlasting, thou art God."

These verses show God as eternal and self-existent, not created or dependent.

Think It Through

- How is a personal God different from a vague higher power?
- Why does it matter whether God depends on the world or the world depends on God?
- How might this view of God affect how someone thinks about meaning and purpose?

WEEK 7 - WHY DO CHRISTIANS BELIEVE GOD CREATED EVERYTHING?

The Big Question

Why does it matter where the world came from? Does believing God created everything actually change anything about life now?

Many people think creation is only about how things started. Christianity treats it as much more than a starting point. It sees creation as something that explains meaning, value, and purpose.

The Christian Answer

Christianity teaches that God created everything on purpose.

This means the world is not an accident and human life is not random. According to Christianity, creation reflects intention. Things exist because God wanted them to exist, not because of chance or necessity.

Creation also explains why the world has order and meaning. If God created the world, then the world is understandable and purposeful. Nature is not just something humans happen to live in. It is something that was designed to function in a certain way.

Christianity also teaches that creation belongs to God. Because God made everything, nothing exists independently of him. This includes human beings. Life is not owned by individuals alone. It is received.

Believing God created everything also shapes responsibility. If the world is created, then it matters how people treat it and how they live within it. Creation is not disposable. It has value because it comes from God.

What the Bible Says (KJV)

Genesis 1:31

"And God saw every thing that he had made, and, behold, it was very good. And the evening and the morning were the sixth day."

Colossians 1:16

"For by him were all things created, that are in heaven, and that are in earth, visible and invisible, whether they be thrones, or dominions, or principalities, or powers: all things were created by him, and for him."

These verses show creation as intentional, good, and connected to God's purpose.

Think It Through

- How does believing the world was created on purpose change the way someone sees life?
- What difference is there between owning life and receiving it?
- Why might creation matter beyond the question of origins?

WEEK 8 - WHAT IS GOD LIKE?

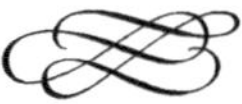

The Big Question

If God is real, what is he actually like? Is God mostly powerful, mostly kind, or something else entirely?

People often imagine God based on feelings or experiences. Some picture God as distant and strict. Others imagine a loving presence with no authority. Christianity claims that God can be known, not guessed.

The Christian Answer

Christianity teaches that God has a real and consistent character.

The Bible describes God using qualities that help explain who he is. Christians often call these qualities God's attributes. They include things like goodness, truth, justice, mercy, and love. These are not separate parts of God. They describe one unified character.

Christianity also teaches that God's power and goodness are not in conflict. God is not loving sometimes and just at other times. He is always fully himself. This means his actions are never random or inconsistent with his character.

Because God does not change, Christians believe they can trust who he is. God's character is not shaped by moods or circumstances. What he was like in the past is what he is like now.

Understanding God's character matters because it shapes how

Christians understand everything else. How someone views God affects how they understand morality, meaning, and hope.

What the Bible Says (KJV)

Psalm 145:8–9

"The Lord is gracious, and full of compassion; slow to anger, and of great mercy.

The Lord is good to all: and his tender mercies are over all his works."

1 John 4:8

"He that loveth not knoweth not God; for God is love."

These verses describe God as both good and loving, not distant or unpredictable.

Think It Through

- Why do people often create their own ideas of what God is like?
- How might believing God's character is consistent change trust or doubt?
- Which of God's qualities do you find hardest to understand, and why?

WEEK 9 - WHAT IS THE TRINITY?

The Big Question

How can Christians believe there is one God but also say the Father, Son, and Holy Spirit are all God? Isn't that a contradiction?

The Trinity is one of the most confusing ideas in Christianity. Many people think it sounds impossible or unnecessary. Christianity claims it is neither made up nor optional.

The Christian Answer

Christianity teaches that there is one God who exists as three distinct persons: the Father, the Son, and the Holy Spirit.

This does not mean there are three gods. It also does not mean God changes forms or plays different roles. Christianity says God is one in being and three in person. The Father is not the Son. The Son is not the Spirit. Yet all three fully share the same divine nature.

Christians did not invent the Trinity to make God more complicated. The idea comes from trying to be faithful to everything the Bible says about God. Scripture speaks of one God. It also speaks of the Father as God, Jesus as God, and the Holy Spirit as God. The Trinity is the way Christianity holds all of that together without ignoring any part.

The Trinity also explains how God can be loving by nature. Love requires relationship. Christianity teaches that relationship has always existed within God himself. God did not need to create in order to love.

The Trinity is not meant to be fully understood. It is meant to be true. Christianity teaches that God is greater than human understanding, yet still knowable in what he has revealed.

What the Bible Says (KJV)

Matthew 28:19

"Go ye therefore, and teach all nations, baptizing them in the name of the Father, and of the Son, and of the Holy Ghost."

2 Corinthians 13:14

"The grace of the Lord Jesus Christ, and the love of God, and the communion of the Holy Ghost, be with you all. Amen."

These verses show the Father, Son, and Holy Spirit spoken of together as fully divine.

Think It Through

- Why do you think Christianity keeps this belief even though it is difficult to understand?
- What problems might arise if Christians ignored parts of what the Bible says about God?
- How does the idea of relationship within God affect how you think about love?

WEEK 10 - WHY DOES THE TRINITY MATTER?

The Big Question

If the Trinity is so hard to understand, why does it matter at all? Isn't it just a technical idea that doesn't affect real life?

Some people think the Trinity is only for theologians. Christianity claims it matters because it shapes how God is understood and how Christians relate to him.

The Christian Answer

Christianity teaches that the Trinity matters because it tells us who God truly is.

If God were only one person, then love would be something God learned or needed later. Christianity teaches that love has always existed within God himself. The Father, Son, and Holy Spirit have always existed in relationship. This means love is not something God started doing. It is who God is.

The Trinity also explains how God can be both close and powerful. The Father sends the Son. The Son enters the world. The Holy Spirit works within people. Christianity teaches that God is not distant from human life. He is involved, personal, and active.

Understanding the Trinity also protects other beliefs. Without it, Jesus might be seen as less than God, or the Holy Spirit might be treated as just a force. The Trinity keeps Christianity from turning Jesus into only a teacher or God into an impersonal power.

Even though the Trinity is difficult, Christianity teaches that truth does not depend on being simple. Some realities are complex because they describe something greater than human experience.

What the Bible Says (KJV)

John 14:9–11

"Jesus saith unto him, Have I been so long time with you, and yet hast thou not known me, Philip? he that hath seen me hath seen the Father; and how sayest thou then, Shew us the Father?

Believest thou not that I am in the Father, and the Father in me? the words that I speak unto you I speak not of myself: but the Father that dwelleth in me, he doeth the works."

John 17:24

"Father, I will that they also, whom thou hast given me, be with me where I am; that they may behold my glory, which thou hast given me: for thou lovedst me before the foundation of the world."

These verses show relationship and unity within God, not separation or confusion.

Think It Through

- Why might a complex belief still be important if it is true?
- How does the Trinity shape the way Christians understand love?
- What could be lost if Jesus or the Holy Spirit were not fully God?

WEEK 11 - DOES GOD CONTROL EVERYTHING?

The Big Question

If God is in control, do human choices really matter? Or is everything already decided?

This question comes up whenever people think seriously about God's power. It can feel like control and choice cancel each other out. Christianity claims they do not.

THE CHRISTIAN ANSWER

Christianity teaches that God is sovereign, but human choices are real.

God's control does not mean humans are puppets. Christianity teaches that God rules over the world in a way that includes real decisions, responsibility, and freedom. People make choices, and those choices matter.

At the same time, Christianity teaches that nothing is outside God's authority. God is not reacting to events as they happen. He is not surprised by history. His purposes are not threatened by human failure or success.

This creates tension, but not contradiction. Christianity does not fully explain how God's control and human choice fit together. It teaches both because Scripture teaches both. Removing either one causes problems. Without God's control, hope becomes uncertain. Without human responsibility, meaning disappears.

Christianity claims that God's rule is not cold or mechanical. It is personal and purposeful. God's control is connected to wisdom and care, not force.

What the Bible Says (KJV)

Proverbs 16:9

"A man's heart deviseth his way: but the Lord directeth his steps."

Romans 8:28

"And we know that all things work together for good to them that love God, to them who are the called according to his purpose."

These verses show both human planning and God's direction working together.

Think It Through

- Why do people often think control and choice cannot exist together?
- How might belief in God's control affect fear or trust?
- What problems arise if either God's control or human responsibility is ignored?

WEEK 12 - CAN HUMANS CHOOSE FREELY?

The Big Question

If God is in control, are people actually free to choose, or are choices just an illusion?

This question often follows naturally from thinking about God's power. If God rules everything, it can feel like human freedom disappears. Christianity says freedom still matters, but it understands it in a specific way.

The Christian Answer

Christianity teaches that humans are responsible for their choices, even under God's authority.

People make real decisions every day. They choose what to believe, how to act, and what to value. Christianity treats these choices as meaningful and accountable. Humans are not excused from responsibility by God's rule.

At the same time, Christianity teaches that human freedom is limited. People are not free in every possible sense. Choices are shaped by nature, desires, and circumstances. Freedom does not mean total independence. It means acting according to what a person truly wants.

Christianity also teaches that sin affects freedom. People are not neutral decision-makers. Their desires are bent, which influences their choices. This is why Christianity says people need help, not just information.

Human freedom and God's authority exist together. Christianity does not reduce one to protect the other. Instead, it holds both as true, even when the full explanation is beyond human understanding.

What the Bible Says (KJV)

Deuteronomy 30:19

"I call heaven and earth to record this day against you, that I have set before you life and death, blessing and cursing: therefore choose life, that both thou and thy seed may live."

Galatians 5:13

"For, brethren, ye have been called unto liberty; only use not liberty for an occasion to the flesh, but by love serve one another."

These verses show both choice and responsibility within God's guidance.

Think It Through

- What does it mean to be responsible for a choice?
- How might desires influence freedom more than rules do?
- Why would Christianity say people need help to choose well?

WEEK 13 - HOW DOES GOD ACT IN THE WORLD?

The Big Question

If God created the world and is in control, how does he actually act in everyday life? Does God still do anything now?

Some people imagine God only acting in the past. Others think God intervenes constantly in obvious ways. Christianity claims God is active, but not always in the ways people expect.

THE CHRISTIAN ANSWER

Christianity teaches that God is continually involved in the world he created.

God's action is not limited to miracles or dramatic moments. Christianity teaches that God sustains the world, guides events, and works through ordinary processes. Life continues because God wills it to continue.

At the same time, Christianity teaches that God can act in direct and noticeable ways. Miracles are not seen as violations of reality, but as acts of the same God who created reality in the first place. God is not bound by the natural order because he is the source of it.

Christianity also teaches that God works through people. Choices, actions, and relationships matter. God's activity does not cancel human responsibility. Instead, it often works through it.

Prayer is one of the ways Christianity understands God's ongoing action. Christians believe prayer is not just self-reflection. It is communication with a real God who hears and responds according to his wisdom.

What the Bible Says (KJV)

Matthew 6:26

"Behold the fowls of the air: for they sow not, neither do they reap, nor gather into barns; yet your heavenly Father feedeth them. Are ye not much better than they?"

James 5:16

"The effectual fervent prayer of a righteous man availeth much."

These verses show God's care for creation and his involvement through prayer.

Think It Through

- Why might God's activity be easy to miss if it is often ordinary?
- How does believing God works through people affect responsibility?
- What difference is there between believing God is distant and believing God is involved?

PART III
HUMANITY AND SIN

WEEK 14 - WHAT ARE HUMAN BEINGS?

The Big Question

Are humans just another part of nature, or is there something different about people compared to everything else?

Many views of the world treat humans as advanced animals or accidental products of nature. Christianity makes a stronger claim about what human beings are and why they matter.

The Christian Answer

Christianity teaches that human beings are created in the image of God.

This does not mean humans look like God physically. It means people reflect God in unique ways. Christianity teaches that humans are capable of reason, creativity, moral judgment, and relationship in a way the rest of creation is not.

Being made in God's image also means humans have dignity that does not depend on ability, success, or usefulness. Value is not earned. It is given. According to Christianity, every person matters because every person is created by God.

Christianity also teaches that humans are both physical and spiritual. People are not just minds trapped in bodies, and they are not only biological machines. Human life includes thought, emotion, will, and responsibility.

Because of this, Christianity treats human life as meaningful from beginning to end. People are not replaceable parts in a system. They are individuals with purpose.

What the Bible Says (KJV)

Genesis 1:26–27

"And God said, Let us make man in our image, after our likeness: and let them have dominion over the fish of the sea, and over the fowl of the air, and over the cattle, and over all the earth, and over every creeping thing that creepeth upon the earth.

So God created man in his own image, in the image of God created he him; male and female created he them."

Psalm 8:4–6

"What is man, that thou art mindful of him? and the son of man, that thou visitest him?

For thou hast made him a little lower than the angels, and hast crowned him with glory and honour.

Thou madest him to have dominion over the works of thy hands; thou hast put all things under his feet."

These verses describe humans as intentionally created and given unique value and responsibility.

Think It Through

- Why does it matter whether human value is earned or given?
- How might viewing people as made in God's image change how others are treated?
- What problems arise if humans are seen as only biological accidents?

WEEK 15 - WHY DO HUMAN BEINGS MATTER?

The Big Question

Do people have value just because they exist, or does value depend on what someone can do, achieve, or contribute?

Many messages today connect worth to success, talent, or usefulness. Christianity makes a different claim about why human life matters.

The Christian Answer

Christianity teaches that human value comes from God, not from performance.

Because humans are created by God and made in his image, their worth is not something they earn. It exists before achievement, ability, or recognition. According to Christianity, a person matters simply because God created them.

This means value does not disappear when someone is weak, failing, or unseen. It does not increase when someone becomes successful or powerful. Human worth remains constant because its source does not change.

Christianity also teaches that this value applies to every person equally. Age, strength, intelligence, and background do not determine importance. All people stand on the same ground before God.

This belief shapes how Christians understand justice, care, and responsibility. If every person has value given by God, then how people treat one another matters deeply. No one is disposable or replaceable.

WHAT THE BIBLE Says (KJV)

Matthew 10:29–31

"Are not two sparrows sold for a farthing? and one of them shall not fall on the ground without your Father.

But the very hairs of your head are all numbered.

Fear ye not therefore, ye are of more value than many sparrows."

James 3:9

"Therewith bless we God, even the Father; and therewith curse we men, which are made after the similitude of God."

These verses show human value as something God knows and assigns, not something people measure.

THINK It Through

- Why do people often connect worth to success or ability?
- How would it change things if value could not be lost or increased?
- What responsibilities come with believing every person has equal worth?

WEEK 16 - WHAT WENT WRONG?

The Big Question

If the world was created good and people have value, why does so much feel broken?

Pain, injustice, and failure are everywhere. Christianity does not deny this. It offers an explanation for why the world does not look the way it was meant to.

THE CHRISTIAN ANSWER

Christianity teaches that something went wrong at the beginning of human history.

The Bible describes a moment when humans chose to reject God's authority and trust their own judgment instead. This choice is called sin. It was not a small mistake. It was a break in the relationship between God and humanity.

According to Christianity, sin did not just affect individual people. It affected everything. Human hearts were changed, relationships were damaged, and the world itself was affected. Brokenness became part of everyday life.

This explains why good intentions do not always lead to good outcomes. It explains why systems fail and why people hurt one another even when they know better. Christianity says the problem is not only outside of us. It is also inside us.

Because of this, Christianity does not believe education, effort, or progress alone can fix what is broken. The problem is deeper than behavior. It is a condition that affects everyone.

What the Bible Says (KJV)

Genesis 3:1–7

"Now the serpent was more subtil than any beast of the field which the Lord God had made. And he said unto the woman, Yea, hath God said, Ye shall not eat of every tree of the garden?

And the woman said unto the serpent, We may eat of the fruit of the trees of the garden:

But of the fruit of the tree which is in the midst of the garden, God hath said, Ye shall not eat of it, neither shall ye touch it, lest ye die.

And the serpent said unto the woman, Ye shall not surely die:

For God doth know that in the day ye eat thereof, then your eyes shall be opened, and ye shall be as gods, knowing good and evil.

And when the woman saw that the tree was good for food, and that it was pleasant to the eyes, and a tree to be desired to make one wise, she took of the fruit thereof, and did eat, and gave also unto her husband with her; and he did eat."

Romans 5:12

"Wherefore, as by one man sin entered into the world, and death by sin; and so death passed upon all men, for that all have sinned."

These passages describe how human choice led to separation from God and lasting brokenness.

Think It Through

- Why do people often blame only systems or circumstances for what goes wrong?
- How does the idea of sin explain both personal and global problems?
- Why might a deeper problem require more than self-improvement to fix?

WEEK 17 - WHAT IS SIN?

The Big Question

Is sin just doing bad things, or does Christianity mean something deeper by it?

People often think of sin as breaking rules. Christianity uses the word in a broader way that explains why brokenness keeps repeating itself.

The Christian Answer

Christianity teaches that sin is more than bad behavior. It is a condition that affects human nature.

Sin includes actions, but it starts deeper than actions. It involves desires, attitudes, and decisions that turn away from God. Christianity teaches that people do not only sin because they make mistakes. They sin because something inside them is misaligned.

This is why simply knowing what is right does not always lead to doing what is right. The problem is not a lack of information. It is a problem of the heart. Christianity says sin shapes what people want, not just what they do.

Christianity also teaches that sin affects relationships. It damages a person's relationship with God, with others, and even with themselves. Sin isolates, distorts, and separates.

Because sin is deeper than behavior, Christianity does not treat it as something that can be solved by effort alone. Rules can restrain actions, but they cannot fix desires. That is why Christianity looks for a deeper solution.

What the Bible Says (KJV)

Romans 3:23

"For all have sinned, and come short of the glory of God."

1 John 1:8

"If we say that we have no sin, we deceive ourselves, and the truth is not in us."

These verses show sin as a universal condition, not just a list of mistakes.

Think It Through

- Why do people often reduce sin to behavior instead of condition?
- How does sin affecting desires explain repeated patterns of failure?
- What limits exist if rules are the only way to deal with sin?

WEEK 18 - WHY CAN'T HUMANS FIX THIS ON THEIR OWN?

The Big Question

If people know what is wrong, why can't they just change and fix the problem themselves?

Many believe that progress, education, or effort will eventually solve what is broken. Christianity agrees those things matter, but it claims they are not enough.

THE CHRISTIAN ANSWER

Christianity teaches that the problem of sin is deeper than effort can reach.

People can improve behavior, learn better habits, and build stronger systems. But Christianity says these changes do not fix the core issue. Sin affects desires, motivations, and direction, not just actions.

Because of this, trying harder does not solve the problem. A person can know what is right and still want what is wrong. Christianity teaches that the will itself needs healing, not just instruction.

This is why Christianity says salvation cannot be earned. If humans could fix themselves, there would be no need for rescue. The Christian message is not "try harder," but "you need help."

This does not mean human effort is meaningless. It means effort has limits. Christianity teaches that true change requires something outside of humanity to intervene and restore what is broken.

What the Bible Says (KJV)

Isaiah 64:6

"But we are all as an unclean thing, and all our righteousnesses are as filthy rags; and we all do fade as a leaf; and our iniquities, like the wind, have taken us away."

Ephesians 2:8–9

"For by grace are ye saved through faith; and that not of yourselves: it is the gift of God:

Not of works, lest any man should boast."

These verses show that human effort alone cannot produce restoration.

Think It Through

- Why do people often believe effort alone should be enough?
- How does the idea of limits change the way failure is understood?
- What difference is there between improvement and restoration?

WEEK 19 - WHAT ABOUT GUILT AND SHAME?

The Big Question

Why do people feel guilt or shame even when no one else knows what they have done?

Guilt and shame are experiences nearly everyone recognizes. Some try to ignore them. Others feel crushed by them. Christianity treats these feelings as signs pointing to something deeper.

The Christian Answer

Christianity teaches that guilt and shame are connected but not the same.

Guilt has to do with responsibility. It comes from knowing that something is wrong and that a choice was made. Christianity says guilt exists because humans are moral beings. People are not just reacting to instincts. They know right from wrong.

Shame goes deeper than guilt. Shame is not just about what someone has done. It is about how someone sees themselves. It says, "Something is wrong with me." Christianity teaches that shame grows out of broken relationship, especially separation from God.

Christianity does not say guilt and shame are illusions. It says they point to a real problem. At the same time, it does not leave people stuck in them. Christianity claims that guilt can be forgiven and shame can be covered and removed.

This is why Christianity speaks so often about forgiveness and restoration. The goal is not denial or self-punishment. It is healing and reconciliation.

What the Bible Says (KJV)

Psalm 32:3–5

"When I kept silence, my bones waxed old through my roaring all the day long.

For day and night thy hand was heavy upon me: my moisture is turned into the drought of summer. Selah.

I acknowledged my sin unto thee, and mine iniquity have I not hid. I said, I will confess my transgressions unto the Lord; and thou forgavest the iniquity of my sin. Selah."

Romans 8:1

"There is therefore now no condemnation to them which are in Christ Jesus, who walk not after the flesh, but after the Spirit."

These verses show guilt acknowledged, forgiveness given, and condemnation removed.

Think It Through

- How is feeling guilty different from feeling ashamed?
- Why might shame be harder to deal with than guilt?
- What would it mean for guilt to be forgiven instead of ignored?

WEEK 20 - WHY IS DEATH SUCH A BIG DEAL?

The Big Question

Why does Christianity talk so much about death? Isn't death just a natural part of life?

Many people treat death as something normal and unavoidable. Christianity agrees that death is common, but it does not treat it as normal in the way it was meant to be.

The Christian Answer

Christianity teaches that death matters because it was not part of God's original design.

According to Christianity, death entered the world as a result of sin. It represents separation. Physical death separates the body from life. Spiritual death separates people from God. This is why death feels wrong even though it is familiar.

Christianity also teaches that death exposes the limits of human control. No amount of knowledge, progress, or effort can ultimately stop it. This is why death creates fear, grief, and urgency. It reminds people that life is fragile.

At the same time, Christianity does not treat death as the final word. It claims that death is an enemy, not a doorway to nothing. Because of this, Christianity takes death seriously without treating it as ultimate.

This is why the Christian message focuses so strongly on rescue and restoration. If death is real and powerful, then the solution must be just as real.

What the Bible Says (KJV)

Romans 6:23

"For the wages of sin is death; but the gift of God is eternal life through Jesus Christ our Lord."

Hebrews 9:27

"And as it is appointed unto men once to die, but after this the judgment."

These verses connect death to sin and point beyond death to accountability and life.

Think It Through

- Why does death feel wrong even though it happens to everyone?
- How does death reveal the limits of human control?
- What difference does it make if death is not the final word?

WEEK 21 - WHY DOES EVIL EXIST?

The Big Question

If God is good and powerful, why is there so much evil in the world?

This question sits behind a lot of doubt and anger. People look at suffering, violence, and injustice and wonder whether a good God can really exist alongside them.

The Christian Answer

Christianity teaches that evil exists because the world is broken, not because God is weak or uncaring.

According to Christianity, God created the world good. Evil did not come from God's character. It entered the world through human rebellion. When humans turned away from God, the effects reached far beyond individual choices. Relationships, systems, and even creation itself were affected.

Christianity also teaches that much of the evil people experience comes directly from human actions. Violence, injustice, and cruelty are not accidents. They are the result of choices made by people who misuse freedom. God allowing choice does not mean God approves of what people do with it.

At the same time, Christianity recognizes that suffering is not always the result of personal wrongdoing. Living in a fallen world means pain can come without clear reasons. Christianity does not pretend to explain every case of suffering. It claims to explain why suffering exists at all.

Most importantly, Christianity teaches that God does not stand outside of suffering. God enters it. The Christian message does not say God ignores evil. It says God acts to defeat it, even at great cost.

What the Bible Says (KJV)

Genesis 6:5

"And God saw that the wickedness of man was great in the earth, and that every imagination of the thoughts of his heart was only evil continually."

Romans 8:20–22

"For the creature was made subject to vanity, not willingly, but by reason of him who hath subjected the same in hope,

Because the creature itself also shall be delivered from the bondage of corruption into the glorious liberty of the children of God.

For we know that the whole creation groaneth and travaileth in pain together until now."

These verses show evil as real and widespread, but not permanent or final.

Think It Through

- Why do people often blame God for evil rather than human choices?
- How does the idea of a broken world explain both personal and natural suffering?
- What difference does it make if evil is temporary rather than permanent?

PART IV
JESUS AND SALVATION

WEEK 22 - WHO IS JESUS?

The Big Question

Was Jesus just a good teacher, or was he something more?

Many people respect Jesus without really knowing who Christianity says he is. Some see him as a moral example. Others see him as a religious leader. Christianity makes a much stronger claim.

The Christian Answer

Christianity teaches that Jesus is both fully God and fully human.

Jesus is not understood as a prophet who pointed to God and then stepped aside. Christianity claims that God entered the world in the person of Jesus. He experienced real human life, including hunger, pain, and death, without stopping being God.

This belief matters because it explains how God can be close to humanity without losing authority. Jesus does not speak about God from a distance. He reveals God from the inside of human life. What Jesus says and does shows what God is like.

Christianity also teaches that Jesus' identity explains his authority. He does not only teach wisdom. He forgives sins, claims divine authority, and accepts worship. These actions only make sense if Jesus is more than a teacher.

If Jesus were only a good man, Christianity would collapse. The faith depends on the claim that Jesus is who he said he was.

What the Bible Says (KJV)

John 1:14

"And the Word was made flesh, and dwelt among us, (and we beheld his glory, the glory as of the only begotten of the Father,) full of grace and truth."

Colossians 2:9

"For in him dwelleth all the fulness of the Godhead bodily."

These verses describe Jesus as God present in human form, not a symbol or idea.

Think It Through

- Why do people often want to reduce Jesus to only a teacher?
- How does Jesus being both God and human change what his life means?
- What would Christianity lose if Jesus were not fully God?

WEEK 23 - WHY DID JESUS COME?

The Big Question

If God wanted to help humanity, why did he send Jesus? What problem was Jesus actually meant to solve?

Some people think Jesus came mainly to teach kindness or inspire better behavior. Christianity claims his purpose was much deeper and more specific than that.

The Christian Answer

Christianity teaches that Jesus came to rescue humanity, not just to instruct it.

According to Christianity, the main problem facing humans is separation from God caused by sin. Teaching alone cannot fix that separation. Christianity claims Jesus came to deal directly with the root of the problem, not just its symptoms.

Jesus' life shows what humans were meant to be. His teaching explains God's will. But his mission goes beyond example and instruction. Christianity teaches that Jesus came to restore the broken relationship between God and humanity.

This is why Jesus speaks so often about being sent. He describes himself as fulfilling a purpose given by the Father. His actions, suffering, and death are all connected to that mission. Christianity does not treat Jesus' death as an accident. It sees it as central.

In short, Christianity teaches that Jesus came to do what humans could not do for themselves: to bring forgiveness, reconciliation, and new life.

What the Bible Says (KJV)

Luke 19:10

"For the Son of man is come to seek and to save that which was lost."

John 3:16

"For God so loved the world, that he gave his only begotten Son, that whosoever believeth in him should not perish, but have everlasting life."

These verses show Jesus' mission as intentional, loving, and focused on rescue.

Think It Through

- Why might teaching alone be insufficient to fix deeper problems?
- What does it mean to be "lost" in the way Christianity describes?
- How does purpose change the way Jesus' life and death are understood?

WEEK 24 - WHAT DID JESUS TEACH?

The Big Question

What was Jesus actually trying to communicate? Was his message mainly about being kind, or was there something deeper?

Many people summarize Jesus' teaching as moral advice. Christianity says his message was centered on something much bigger than behavior.

THE CHRISTIAN ANSWER

Christianity teaches that Jesus' central message was about the kingdom of God.

When Jesus spoke, he was not only giving instructions for better living. He was announcing that God's rule was breaking into the world. The kingdom of God refers to God's authority being made visible and active in human life.

Jesus taught that the kingdom was not mainly political or military. It was not about power the way people usually understand it. It involved repentance, trust, and a changed way of seeing reality. Jesus called people to recognize God's rule and respond to it.

His teachings also showed what life looks like under God's rule. He spoke about love, humility, forgiveness, and obedience. These were not random moral ideas. They flowed from the reality that God is king.

Christianity teaches that Jesus' teaching only makes full sense when connected to who he is. He did not just explain the kingdom. He claimed to bring it.

What the Bible Says (KJV)

Mark 1:15

"And saying, The time is fulfilled, and the kingdom of God is at hand: repent ye, and believe the gospel."

Matthew 5:17

"Think not that I am come to destroy the law, or the prophets: I am not come to destroy, but to fulfil."

These verses show Jesus announcing God's kingdom and fulfilling what came before him.

Think It Through

- How is the idea of God's kingdom different from just moral advice?
- Why would Jesus' teaching depend on who he is, not just what he said?
- What might change if someone believed God's rule was real and present?

WEEK 25 - WHY DID JESUS DIE?

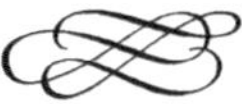

The Big Question

If Jesus came to bring life and healing, why did his story end with a violent death?

For many people, the cross is confusing. It can look like a failure or a tragedy. Christianity claims it was neither accidental nor meaningless.

The Christian Answer

Christianity teaches that Jesus died on purpose.

According to Christianity, Jesus' death was not the result of bad luck or poor planning. It was central to his mission. The cross is where the problem of sin is dealt with directly.

Christianity teaches that sin separates humans from God and brings real consequences. Justice cannot simply be ignored. The cross is where Jesus takes that burden on himself. He stands in place of sinners and absorbs what separation from God deserves.

This is called atonement. It means that Jesus' death makes forgiveness possible without pretending sin does not matter. God's justice and mercy meet at the cross.

Because of this, the cross is not only about suffering. It is about rescue. Christianity teaches that Jesus' death opens the way for reconciliation between God and humanity.

. . .

What the Bible Says (KJV)

Isaiah 53:5

"But he was wounded for our transgressions, he was bruised for our iniquities: the chastisement of our peace was upon him; and with his stripes we are healed."

Romans 5:8

"But God commendeth his love toward us, in that, while we were yet sinners, Christ died for us."

These verses show Jesus' death as intentional and connected to forgiveness and healing.

Think It Through

- Why might a rescue mission require sacrifice?
- How does the cross show both justice and mercy at the same time?
- Why would forgiveness be costly rather than easy?

WEEK 26 - WHAT HAPPENED ON THE CROSS?

The Big Question

What actually changed when Jesus died on the cross? Was it just an example of love, or did something real happen?

The cross is central to Christianity, but it is often misunderstood. Christianity claims the cross accomplished something, not just symbolized something.

The Christian Answer

Christianity teaches that the cross dealt with sin, guilt, and separation from God.

On the cross, Jesus takes the place of sinners. Christianity teaches that sin carries real consequences, including separation from God. Jesus willingly accepts those consequences so they do not fall on humanity. This is why the cross is described as substitution. Jesus stands in for others.

The cross also cancels guilt. Christianity teaches that sin creates a real debt, not just emotional regret. On the cross, that debt is paid. Forgiveness is not pretending nothing happened. It is the result of the cost being covered.

Christianity also teaches that the cross defeats the power of sin and evil. By submitting to death and then overcoming it, Jesus breaks the hold these forces have over humanity. The cross looks like weakness, but Christianity claims it is victory.

Because of this, the cross is not only about the past. It changes the present and the future. It opens the way for forgiveness, freedom, and restored relationship with God.

What the Bible Says (KJV)

Colossians 2:13–15

"And you, being dead in your sins and the uncircumcision of your flesh, hath he quickened together with him, having forgiven you all trespasses;

Blotting out the handwriting of ordinances that was against us, which was contrary to us, and took it out of the way, nailing it to his cross;

And having spoiled principalities and powers, he made a shew of them openly, triumphing over them in it."

1 Peter 2:24

"Who his own self bare our sins in his own body on the tree, that we, being dead to sins, should live unto righteousness: by whose stripes ye were healed."

These verses describe the cross as forgiveness given, guilt removed, and victory over sin and evil.

Think It Through

- Why is forgiveness more meaningful if a cost is involved?
- How does the idea of substitution change the way responsibility is understood?
- Why might something that looks like weakness actually be strength?

WEEK 27 - DID JESUS REALLY RISE FROM THE DEAD?

The Big Question

Is the resurrection meant to be taken literally, or is it just a symbol for hope or new beginnings?

Many people are comfortable with Jesus' teaching but struggle with the idea of resurrection. Christianity makes a clear claim: it says the resurrection actually happened.

THE CHRISTIAN ANSWER

Christianity teaches that Jesus rose from the dead physically, not symbolically.

The resurrection is not described as a vision, feeling, or metaphor. Christianity claims Jesus' body was truly dead and truly brought back to life. This is why the resurrection is treated as essential, not optional.

According to Christianity, if the resurrection did not happen, then Jesus' death would have no lasting power. Sin would still win, death would still rule, and hope would be wishful thinking. The resurrection is what confirms that the cross worked.

The resurrection also shows that death is not the final authority. Christianity teaches that God has power not only over life but over death itself. This changes how Christians understand fear, suffering, and the future.

Because of this, Christianity does not rest on ideas alone. It rests on an event. The resurrection is the foundation for everything that follows.

What the Bible Says (KJV)

Luke 24:39

"Behold my hands and my feet, that it is I myself: handle me, and see; for a spirit hath not flesh and bones, as ye see me have."

1 Corinthians 15:3–4

"For I delivered unto you first of all that which I also received, how that Christ died for our sins according to the scriptures;

And that he was buried, and that he rose again the third day according to the scriptures."

These verses describe the resurrection as physical, witnessed, and central to Christian belief.

Think It Through

- Why might people prefer a symbolic resurrection over a physical one?
- What difference does it make if the resurrection actually happened?
- How does the resurrection change the way death is viewed?

WEEK 28 - WHAT IS SALVATION?

The Big Question

What does it actually mean to be "saved"? Saved from what, and for what?

The word "salvation" is used a lot in Christianity, but it is often left vague. Christianity gives it a specific meaning tied to real problems and real change.

THE CHRISTIAN ANSWER

Christianity teaches that salvation is rescue.

Salvation means being saved from sin, separation from God, and the power of death. It is not mainly about becoming a better version of yourself. It is about being brought out of a condition you cannot escape on your own.

Christianity also teaches that salvation is relational. It restores the broken relationship between God and humanity. Being saved is not just receiving forgiveness. It is being brought back into connection with God.

Salvation also includes new life. Christianity teaches that God does not only remove guilt. He gives a new direction, new identity, and new future. Salvation is both forgiveness and transformation.

Because of this, salvation is not limited to the moment someone believes. It begins there, but it continues as God reshapes a person's life over time.

What the Bible Says (KJV)

Titus 3:5

"Not by works of righteousness which we have done, but according to his mercy he saved us, by the washing of regeneration, and renewing of the Holy Ghost."

Romans 10:9

"That if thou shalt confess with thy mouth the Lord Jesus, and shalt believe in thine heart that God hath raised him from the dead, thou shalt be saved."

These verses describe salvation as God's work of rescue and renewal, not human achievement.

Think It Through

- Why does Christianity describe salvation as rescue rather than improvement?
- What is the difference between being forgiven and being restored?
- How does thinking of salvation as ongoing change affect expectations?

WEEK 29 - WHAT IS GRACE?

The Big Question

If salvation is a gift, why can't people earn it? Wouldn't effort and good behavior count for something?

Many people assume that rewards should be earned. Christianity teaches something different when it comes to salvation.

THE CHRISTIAN ANSWER

Christianity teaches that grace means receiving what you did not earn.

Grace is God's favor given freely, not as payment for good behavior. Christianity claims that if salvation could be earned, it would no longer be grace. It would be a reward.

This does not mean actions do not matter. It means actions are not the basis of acceptance. Christianity teaches that humans are saved because of what God has done, not because of what they have achieved.

Grace also changes motivation. When acceptance is not something that has to be earned, obedience becomes a response rather than a requirement. Christianity teaches that people obey God not to earn love, but because they have already received it.

Because grace is undeserved, it removes boasting and comparison.

No one can claim superiority. Everyone stands on the same ground, dependent on God's mercy.

What the Bible Says (KJV)

Ephesians 2:8–9

"For by grace are ye saved through faith; and that not of yourselves: it is the gift of God:

Not of works, lest any man should boast."

Romans 11:6

"And if by grace, then is it no more of works: otherwise grace is no more grace. But if it be of works, then is it no more grace: otherwise work is no more work."

These verses clearly separate grace from earning and effort.

Think It Through

- Why do people often struggle with receiving something they did not earn?
- How does grace change the reason behind obedience?
- What problems arise when people compare worth based on effort?

WEEK 30 - WHAT IS FAITH?

The Big Question

Is faith just believing something without evidence, or does Christianity mean something more specific by it?

People often describe faith as a blind leap or a feeling. Christianity uses the word in a more grounded way.

The Christian Answer

Christianity teaches that faith is trust, not blind belief.

Faith is not pretending something is true without reason. It is trusting what God has revealed and promised. Christianity says faith has an object. It is not faith in faith itself. It is trust placed in God and what he has done.

This trust involves the mind and the will. It includes understanding what Christianity claims and choosing to rely on it. Faith is not the opposite of thinking. It is a response to what is believed to be true.

Christianity also teaches that faith is active. It shows itself in how someone lives and what they depend on. Faith does not mean certainty about everything. It means commitment despite uncertainty.

Because of this, Christianity treats faith as essential. It is how people receive what God offers, not something they use to earn it.

• • •

What the Bible Says (KJV)

Hebrews 11:1

"Now faith is the substance of things hoped for, the evidence of things not seen."

John 6:29

"Jesus answered and said unto them, This is the work of God, that ye believe on him whom he hath sent."

These verses describe faith as trust in what God has promised and revealed.

Think It Through

- Why do people often think faith means ignoring questions or doubts?
- How is trust different from certainty?
- What does it mean to place trust in something or someone?

WEEK 31 - CAN SOMEONE BE SURE THEY ARE SAVED?

The Big Question

If salvation is based on faith and grace, can someone really know they are saved, or is it always uncertain?

Some people live with constant doubt. Others assume certainty without thought. Christianity claims there is a real basis for assurance, not just confidence or fear.

The Christian Answer

Christianity teaches that assurance comes from God's promise, not personal performance.

If salvation depended on perfect behavior, no one could be sure. Christianity teaches that salvation depends on what God has done through Jesus. Because God does not change, his promises can be trusted.

Assurance does not mean a person never struggles or doubts. Christianity recognizes that faith can feel weak at times. Assurance is not about never questioning. It is about knowing where trust is placed.

Christianity also teaches that real faith produces change over time. Obedience and growth do not create assurance, but they support it. They are signs, not the foundation.

Because of this, Christianity holds assurance and humility together. Confidence is grounded in God's faithfulness, not in human success.

What the Bible Says (KJV)

John 10:28

"And I give unto them eternal life; and they shall never perish, neither shall any man pluck them out of my hand."

Philippians 1:6

"Being confident of this very thing, that he which hath begun a good work in you will perform it until the day of Jesus Christ."

These verses point to God's keeping power, not human strength.

Think It Through

- Why might assurance be difficult if it is based on personal effort?
- How does trusting a promise differ from trusting performance?
- What signs might show faith is real without becoming the basis for confidence?

PART V
THE CHRISTIAN LIFE

WEEK 32 - WHAT IS THE CHURCH?

The Big Question

Is the church a building, an event, or an organization, or does Christianity mean something else by it?

Many people associate church with a place or a schedule. Christianity uses the word in a much deeper way.

The Christian Answer

Christianity teaches that the church is not a building but a people.

The church is made up of those who trust in Jesus and belong to him. Buildings, services, and programs exist to support the church, but they are not the church itself. According to Christianity, the church exists wherever believers exist.

Christianity also teaches that the church is meant to be a community, not just a collection of individuals. Faith is personal, but it is not meant to be lived alone. The church exists to encourage, correct, support, and build one another up.

The church also has a purpose. Christianity teaches that the church represents God's work in the world. It exists to worship God, share truth, and live out what it believes.

Because of this, the church is not optional in Christianity. It is not an extra for highly committed believers. It is part of how the Christian faith is meant to function.

What the Bible Says (KJV)

1 Corinthians 12:27

"Now ye are the body of Christ, and members in particular."

Ephesians 2:19

"Now therefore ye are no more strangers and foreigners, but fellow-citizens with the saints, and of the household of God."

These verses describe the church as a living body and a shared family, not a location.

Think It Through

- Why do people often reduce church to a place or event?
- How does seeing the church as a community change responsibility?
- What might be lost if faith is practiced only alone?

WEEK 33 - WHY DO CHRISTIANS GATHER?

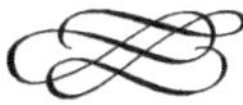

The Big Question

If faith is personal, why do Christians bother meeting together at all?

Some people think belief should stay private. Others see gathering as tradition or habit. Christianity claims there is a deeper reason Christians come together.

THE CHRISTIAN ANSWER

Christianity teaches that gathering strengthens faith and keeps it grounded.

Christians do not gather because God needs attendance. They gather because people need one another. Faith can weaken when it is isolated. Being with others reminds believers of what they share and helps keep belief from drifting.

Gathering also provides encouragement and correction. Christianity does not assume individuals always see clearly on their own. Community helps people stay honest about what they believe and how they live.

Christian gatherings are also meant to focus attention on God. Teaching, prayer, and shared worship help re-center belief and purpose. This is not about performance. It is about alignment.

Because of this, gathering is not treated as optional entertainment. It is part of how Christian belief is sustained over time.

What the Bible Says (KJV)

Hebrews 10:24–25

"And let us consider one another to provoke unto love and to good works:

Not forsaking the assembling of ourselves together, as the manner of some is; but exhorting one another: and so much the more, as ye see the day approaching."

Acts 2:42

"And they continued stedfastly in the apostles' doctrine and fellowship, and in breaking of bread, and in prayers."

These verses show gathering as encouragement, teaching, and shared life.

Think It Through

- Why might faith weaken when it is practiced alone?
- How can community help both belief and behavior?
- What dangers exist in treating gathering as optional?

WEEK 34 - WHAT IS WORSHIP?

The Big Question

Is worship just singing in church, or does Christianity mean something broader by it?

Many people connect worship only with music or religious events. Christianity uses the word in a much wider way.

The Christian Answer

Christianity teaches that worship is about direction, not just activity.

Worship means recognizing who God is and responding appropriately. Singing can be worship, but worship is not limited to songs. Christianity teaches that worship includes how a person thinks, chooses, and lives.

According to Christianity, everyone worships something. People center their lives around what they value most. Worship happens whenever something takes first place and shapes priorities and decisions.

Christian worship, then, is not about creating a certain feeling. It is about aligning life with God's worth and authority. It includes gratitude, obedience, trust, and attention directed toward God.

Because of this, worship is not confined to a building or a moment. It is meant to shape everyday life.

. . .

What the Bible Says (KJV)

Romans 12:1

"I beseech you therefore, brethren, by the mercies of God, that ye present your bodies a living sacrifice, holy, acceptable unto God, which is your reasonable service."

Psalm 95:6

"O come, let us worship and bow down: let us kneel before the Lord our maker."

These verses show worship as both a response of the heart and a way of living.

Think It Through

- Why do people often limit worship to music or events?
- What kinds of things tend to take first place in people's lives?
- How might everyday choices reflect what someone truly values?

WEEK 35 - WHAT ARE BAPTISM AND COMMUNION?

The Big Question

Why does Christianity include physical practices like baptism and communion? Aren't beliefs supposed to be internal?

Some people see these practices as outdated rituals. Others treat them as symbols without much meaning. Christianity gives them a specific purpose.

The Christian Answer

Christianity teaches that baptism and communion are visible signs of invisible realities.

Baptism represents identification with Jesus. It shows a person's connection to Jesus' death and resurrection. Christianity teaches that baptism does not save someone by itself. It publicly expresses a faith that already exists.

Communion, also called the Lord's Supper, reminds Christians of Jesus' sacrifice. Bread and wine represent his body and blood. Christianity teaches that this practice keeps the focus on the cross and the meaning of forgiveness.

Both practices use physical elements because humans are physical beings. Christianity does not separate belief from the body. These actions involve the whole person, not just thoughts.

Because of this, baptism and communion are not empty rituals. They are meant to teach, remind, and unite believers around shared truth.

What the Bible Says (KJV)

Matthew 28:19

"Go ye therefore, and teach all nations, baptizing them in the name of the Father, and of the Son, and of the Holy Ghost."

1 Corinthians 11:23–26

"For I have received of the Lord that which also I delivered unto you, That the Lord Jesus the same night in which he was betrayed took bread:

And when he had given thanks, he brake it, and said, Take, eat: this is my body, which is broken for you: this do in remembrance of me.

After the same manner also he took the cup, when he had supped, saying, This cup is the new testament in my blood: this do ye, as oft as ye drink it, in remembrance of me.

For as often as ye eat this bread, and drink this cup, ye do shew the Lord's death till he come."

These verses describe baptism and communion as practices tied directly to Jesus' command and sacrifice.

Think It Through

- Why might physical actions help reinforce belief?
- How do symbols help people remember important truths?
- What happens when practices are separated from their meaning?

WEEK 36 - HOW DO CHRISTIANS READ THE BIBLE?

The Big Question

If the Bible matters so much, how are people supposed to read it without misunderstanding it?

People often assume the Bible can mean anything anyone wants it to mean. Others think only experts can understand it. Christianity takes a different approach.

THE CHRISTIAN ANSWER

Christianity teaches that the Bible is meant to be read carefully, not casually or creatively.

Christians believe the Bible has meaning because it was written to communicate truth, not confusion. Reading it well involves paying attention to context, purpose, and the kind of writing being used. History, poetry, letters, and teaching are read differently.

Christianity also teaches that Scripture explains Scripture. Individual verses are not meant to be pulled out and used on their own. Beliefs are formed by looking at the Bible as a whole and letting clearer passages guide harder ones.

At the same time, Christianity teaches that the Bible is not reserved for experts only. It can be understood by ordinary people who read honestly and humbly. The goal is not to force meaning into the text, but to listen to what it is saying.

Because of this, reading the Bible well requires patience and care. It is not about finding personal meaning first. It is about understanding the message that is already there.

What the Bible Says (KJV)

Psalm 119:130

"The entrance of thy words giveth light; it giveth understanding unto the simple."

2 Peter 1:20

"Knowing this first, that no prophecy of the scripture is of any private interpretation."

These verses point to clarity through Scripture itself and warn against twisting meaning.

Think It Through

- Why can taking verses out of context cause problems?
- How is careful reading different from making a text say what you want?
- Why might humility matter when reading something believed to be God's word?

WEEK 37 - WHAT IS PRAYER?

The Big Question

If God already knows everything, why do Christians pray at all?

Prayer can seem pointless or confusing. Some see it as talking to themselves. Others treat it like a way to get what they want. Christianity understands prayer differently.

The Christian Answer

Christianity teaches that prayer is communication, not control.

Prayer is not about informing God or changing his character. It is about relationship. Christians believe prayer is speaking to a real God who listens and responds according to his wisdom.

Prayer also shapes the person who prays. It aligns desires with God's will and helps clarify trust and dependence. Christianity does not treat prayer as a transaction. It is not a way to manipulate outcomes.

At the same time, Christianity teaches that prayer matters. God chooses to work through prayer as part of his involvement in the world. This does not mean prayer overrides God's plans. It means God includes human participation in his purposes.

Because of this, prayer is not a performance or formula. It is honest communication rooted in trust.

. . .

What the Bible Says (KJV)

Matthew 6:9–13

"After this manner therefore pray ye: Our Father which art in heaven, Hallowed be thy name.

Thy kingdom come. Thy will be done in earth, as it is in heaven.

Give us this day our daily bread.

And forgive us our debts, as we forgive our debtors.

And lead us not into temptation, but deliver us from evil:

For thine is the kingdom, and the power, and the glory, for ever. Amen."

Philippians 4:6

"Be careful for nothing; but in every thing by prayer and supplication with thanksgiving let your requests be made known unto God."

These verses show prayer as trustful communication and dependence, not control.

Think It Through

- Why might prayer feel unnecessary if God already knows everything?
- How does prayer change the person who prays, even if circumstances do not change?
- What difference is there between asking and trying to control outcomes?

WEEK 38 - HOW SHOULD CHRISTIANS LIVE?

The Big Question

If Christians are saved by grace, does how they live still matter?

Some people think grace removes responsibility. Others turn Christianity into rule-following. Christianity claims a different relationship between belief and behavior.

The Christian Answer

Christianity teaches that how Christians live matters because belief reshapes life.

Good behavior is not the cause of salvation. It is the result of it. Christianity teaches that when someone is changed by grace, their values and priorities begin to change as well. Obedience flows from relationship, not fear.

Christian living is not about perfection. It is about direction. Growth takes time, and failure still happens. Christianity does not expect instant change. It expects ongoing transformation.

Christianity also teaches that obedience is connected to love. Following God is not meant to be mechanical. It is a response to trust and gratitude. Rules exist, but they are meant to guide life, not replace relationship.

Because of this, Christian living is not about earning approval. It is about reflecting a changed heart.

What the Bible Says (KJV)

John 14:15

"If ye love me, keep my commandments."

Ephesians 2:10

"For we are his workmanship, created in Christ Jesus unto good works, which God hath before ordained that we should walk in them."

These verses connect obedience to love and purpose, not to earning salvation.

Think It Through

- Why do people often separate belief from behavior?
- How is direction different from perfection?
- What motivates obedience when it is not about earning approval?

WEEK 39 - WHAT IS CHRISTIAN LOVE?

The Big Question

Is Christian love just being nice, or does it mean something more demanding?

The word love is used constantly, but it can mean very different things. Christianity gives love a specific shape and standard.

The Christian Answer

Christianity teaches that love is commitment, not just feeling.

Christian love is not defined by emotion alone. Feelings can change. Christianity teaches that love is choosing to seek the good of others, even when it costs something. This kind of love is active, not passive.

Jesus is presented as the model of love. His actions show that love includes truth, sacrifice, and faithfulness. Love does not ignore what is wrong. It aims at restoration, not comfort.

Christianity also teaches that love flows from God's love first. People are not asked to generate love on their own. They respond to the love they have received. This keeps love from becoming performance or self-protection.

Because of this, Christian love is not weak or vague. It is purposeful and often difficult.

. . .

What the Bible Says (KJV)

John 13:34–35

"A new commandment I give unto you, That ye love one another; as I have loved you, that ye also love one another.

By this shall all men know that ye are my disciples, if ye have love one to another."

1 Corinthians 13:4–7

"Charity suffereth long, and is kind; charity envieth not; charity vaunteth not itself, is not puffed up,

Doth not behave itself unseemly, seeketh not her own, is not easily provoked, thinketh no evil;

Rejoiceth not in iniquity, but rejoiceth in the truth;

Beareth all things, believeth all things, hopeth all things, endureth all things."

These verses define love by action, patience, and truth, not just emotion.

Think It Through

- How is commitment different from feeling?
- Why might truth be part of real love rather than opposed to it?
- What makes this kind of love difficult to practice?

WEEK 40 - WHAT IS HOLINESS?

The Big Question

Why does Christianity talk so much about holiness? Does it just mean being morally perfect?

The word holiness often sounds distant or unrealistic. Christianity gives it a specific meaning that is deeper than rule-following.

THE CHRISTIAN ANSWER

Christianity teaches that holiness means being set apart for God.

Holiness is not mainly about avoiding mistakes. It is about belonging. Something is holy when it is devoted to God's purposes. For people, holiness means living in alignment with who God is and what he wants.

Christianity also teaches that holiness is a process. People are not instantly perfected. Growth happens over time as values, desires, and habits are reshaped. Failure does not cancel holiness. Direction matters more than flawlessness.

Holiness is also relational. It grows out of closeness to God, not distance. Christianity does not teach that people become holy by separating themselves from life. It teaches that holiness changes how life is lived.

Because of this, holiness is not about superiority. It is about transformation.

. . .

What the Bible Says (KJV)

1 Peter 1:15–16

"But as he which hath called you is holy, so be ye holy in all manner of conversation;

Because it is written, Be ye holy; for I am holy."

Hebrews 12:14

"Follow peace with all men, and holiness, without which no man shall see the Lord."

These verses connect holiness to God's character and to the way life is lived.

Think It Through

- Why does holiness often get confused with perfection?
- How is being set apart different from being isolated?
- What might change if holiness were seen as belonging rather than rule-keeping?

WEEK 41 - WHAT IS THE HOLY SPIRIT?

The Big Question

Who is the Holy Spirit, and what does he actually do?

The Holy Spirit is often the least understood part of Christianity. Some people think of the Spirit as a force or feeling. Christianity teaches something much more specific.

The Christian Answer

Christianity teaches that the Holy Spirit is God, not an impersonal power.

The Holy Spirit is the third person of the Trinity. He is not energy, emotion, or inspiration. He is fully God and personally active. Christianity teaches that the Spirit works within believers in a unique way.

The Holy Spirit's role includes guiding, convicting, comforting, and strengthening. He helps people understand God's truth and applies it to their lives. Christianity teaches that change from the inside out happens through the Spirit's work, not through willpower alone.

The Spirit also empowers believers to live faithfully. Christianity does not claim people can follow God by effort alone. The Holy Spirit provides help, direction, and endurance.

Because of this, the Christian life is not meant to be lived independently. It is lived with God actively present within believers.

. . .

WHAT THE BIBLE Says (KJV)

John 14:16–17

"And I will pray the Father, and he shall give you another Comforter, that he may abide with you for ever;

Even the Spirit of truth; whom the world cannot receive, because it seeth him not, neither knoweth him: but ye know him; for he dwelleth with you, and shall be in you."

Romans 8:11

"But if the Spirit of him that raised up Jesus from the dead dwell in you, he that raised up Christ from the dead shall also quicken your mortal bodies by his Spirit that dwelleth in you."

These verses describe the Holy Spirit as personal, present, and life-giving.

THINK It Through

• Why might people prefer thinking of the Spirit as a force rather than a person?

• How does the idea of God living within believers change responsibility?

• Why would inner change require help beyond effort?

PART VI
THE FUTURE

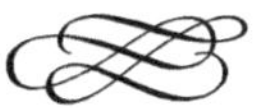

WEEK 42 - HOW DOES THE HOLY SPIRIT CHANGE PEOPLE?

The Big Question

If the Holy Spirit lives within believers, what actually changes in a person's life?

Some expect dramatic experiences. Others expect instant perfection. Christianity teaches a quieter, deeper kind of change.

THE CHRISTIAN ANSWER

Christianity teaches that the Holy Spirit changes people from the inside out.

The Spirit works first at the level of desire and understanding, not just behavior. Christianity teaches that real change begins when what a person loves, trusts, and values starts to shift. Actions follow inner change, not the other way around.

This change is usually gradual. Christianity does not promise instant maturity. Growth takes time, and struggle remains part of the process. The presence of struggle does not mean failure. It often means growth is happening.

The Holy Spirit also brings conviction. This is not meant to shame, but to guide. Conviction helps people recognize what needs to change and where healing is needed. Christianity teaches that conviction leads toward restoration, not rejection.

Because of this, Christian growth is not self-improvement. It is cooperation with God's work within a person.

What the Bible Says (KJV)

Galatians 5:22–23

"But the fruit of the Spirit is love, joy, peace, longsuffering, gentleness, goodness, faith,

Meekness, temperance: against such there is no law."

2 Corinthians 3:18

"But we all, with open face beholding as in a glass the glory of the Lord, are changed into the same image from glory to glory, even as by the Spirit of the Lord."

These verses describe change as fruit and transformation over time, not instant perfection.

Think It Through

- Why might gradual change be more realistic than instant change?
- How is inner change different from behavior control?
- What does cooperation with change look like in everyday life?

WEEK 43 - WHAT IS THE CHRISTIAN LIFE REALLY ABOUT?

The Big Question

Is Christianity mainly about rules, beliefs, or something else entirely?

Some people experience Christianity as pressure. Others see it as just ideas. Christianity claims it is about a whole way of life shaped by relationship.

THE CHRISTIAN ANSWER

Christianity teaches that the Christian life is about following Jesus.

At its core, Christianity is not about mastering rules or collecting correct beliefs. It is about trust and direction. To follow Jesus means shaping life around who he is, what he taught, and what he has done.

This includes beliefs, actions, and attitudes. Christianity does not separate these. What someone believes affects how they live. How they live reveals what they trust. The Christian life is meant to be consistent, not compartmentalized.

Christianity also teaches that following Jesus is ongoing. It is not a one-time decision. Growth, correction, and learning continue throughout life. Failure does not end the journey. Repentance and grace keep it moving forward.

Because of this, Christianity is not about perfection. It is about alignment. The goal is not to look religious, but to live faithfully.

What the Bible Says (KJV)

Matthew 16:24

"Then said Jesus unto his disciples, If any man will come after me, let him deny himself, and take up his cross, and follow me."

John 12:26

"If any man serve me, let him follow me; and where I am, there shall also my servant be: if any man serve me, him will my Father honour."

These verses describe Christianity as a call to follow, not just to believe.

Think It Through

- Why do people often reduce Christianity to rules or ideas?
- How is following different from simply agreeing?
- What does alignment look like in daily life?

WEEK 44 - WHAT IS REPENTANCE?

The Big Question

If Christians are forgiven, why do they still need repentance?

Repentance often sounds negative or shame-based. Christianity gives it a different meaning tied to honesty and change.

The Christian Answer

Christianity teaches that repentance means turning, not groveling.

Repentance is not about self-hatred or punishment. It is about recognizing when life has moved out of alignment with God and choosing to turn back. Christianity treats repentance as part of a healthy relationship, not a one-time requirement.

Repentance involves both the mind and the direction of life. It includes admitting what is wrong and choosing a different path. Christianity teaches that repentance is ongoing because growth is ongoing.

Forgiveness does not make repentance unnecessary. It makes it possible. Because forgiveness is real, repentance does not lead to rejection. It leads to restoration.

This is why repentance is not opposed to grace. It depends on grace.

What the Bible Says (KJV)

Acts 3:19

"Repent ye therefore, and be converted, that your sins may be blotted out, when the times of refreshing shall come from the presence of the Lord."

2 Corinthians 7:10

"For godly sorrow worketh repentance to salvation not to be repented of: but the sorrow of the world worketh death."

These verses describe repentance as leading to renewal, not despair.

Think It Through

- Why might repentance feel threatening rather than freeing?
- How is turning different from self-punishment?
- What role does honesty play in real change?

WEEK 45 - WHAT IS FORGIVENESS?

The Big Question

If forgiveness is offered freely, does that mean what happened does not matter anymore?

Forgiveness is often confused with ignoring harm or pretending pain never happened. Christianity defines it more carefully.

The Christian Answer

Christianity teaches that forgiveness is releasing a debt, not denying a wrong.

Forgiveness does not say that something was acceptable. It says that payment will not be demanded from the offender. Christianity treats forgiveness as a costly choice, not an emotional shortcut.

Because forgiveness is rooted in what Jesus has done, Christians forgive not because hurt is small, but because grace is greater. Forgiveness flows from having been forgiven first. It is not about fairness. It is about freedom.

Christianity also teaches that forgiveness does not always mean immediate trust or restored relationship. Trust can take time. Boundaries can remain. Forgiveness addresses the heart, not every consequence.

This is why forgiveness is difficult. It requires letting go of control and the right to revenge. Christianity claims this is only possible through God's grace.

What the Bible Says (KJV)

Matthew 18:21–22

"Then came Peter to him, and said, Lord, how oft shall my brother sin against me, and I forgive him? till seven times?

Jesus saith unto him, I say not unto thee, Until seven times: but, Until seventy times seven."

Ephesians 4:32

"And be ye kind one to another, tenderhearted, forgiving one another, even as God for Christ's sake hath forgiven you."

These verses connect forgiveness directly to God's forgiveness first.

Think It Through

- Why is forgiveness often mistaken for excusing harm?
- How does forgiveness free the one who forgives?
- What is the difference between forgiveness and trust?

WEEK 46 - HOW SHOULD CHRISTIANS TREAT OTHERS?

The Big Question

If Christians believe what they believe, how should that actually show up in how they treat people?

Beliefs always shape behavior. Christianity claims that faith is meant to be visible, especially in relationships.

The Christian Answer

Christianity teaches that how Christians treat others reflects how they understand God.

Jesus teaches that love for God and love for others are inseparable. Treatment of people is not a side issue. It is a direct expression of faith. Christianity does not allow belief to stay abstract.

This includes kindness, patience, honesty, and humility. It also includes loving people who are difficult, different, or opposed. Christianity does not teach love based on agreement or convenience.

Christians are also called to treat others with dignity because every person is made in God's image. This applies regardless of belief, behavior, or background. Respect is not earned. It is given.

Because of this, Christian behavior toward others becomes a test of whether belief is real or merely spoken.

. . .

What the Bible Says (KJV)

Matthew 22:37–39

"Jesus said unto him, Thou shalt love the Lord thy God with all thy heart, and with all thy soul, and with all thy mind.

This is the first and great commandment.

And the second is like unto it, Thou shalt love thy neighbour as thyself."

Micah 6:8

"He hath shewed thee, O man, what is good; and what doth the Lord require of thee, but to do justly, and to love mercy, and to walk humbly with thy God?"

These verses connect belief directly to how people are treated.

Think It Through

- Why is it easier to claim belief than to live it out?
- How does seeing others as made in God's image change behavior?
- What challenges come with loving people who disagree or hurt you?

WEEK 47 - WHAT IS MISSION?

The Big Question

Is Christianity meant to be kept private, or is it supposed to be shared?

Some people think faith should stay personal. Others think sharing faith means pressure or arguments. Christianity understands mission in a specific way.

THE CHRISTIAN ANSWER

Christianity teaches that mission means representing Jesus in the world.

Mission is not mainly about winning arguments or forcing belief. It is about living and speaking in a way that points to who Jesus is and what he has done. Christianity teaches that believers are sent into everyday life as witnesses, not salespeople.

This includes words and actions. Christians are called to speak truth honestly and to live in a way that reflects love, integrity, and hope. Mission happens through relationships, service, and faithfulness, not just public moments.

Christianity also teaches that mission flows from gratitude, not obligation. People share what they believe matters. Mission is a response to having received grace, not a requirement to earn approval.

Because of this, mission is not reserved for experts or leaders. It is part of ordinary Christian life.

What the Bible Says (KJV)

Matthew 28:19–20

"Go ye therefore, and teach all nations, baptizing them in the name of the Father, and of the Son, and of the Holy Ghost:

Teaching them to observe all things whatsoever I have commanded you: and, lo, I am with you alway, even unto the end of the world. Amen."

1 Peter 3:15

"But sanctify the Lord God in your hearts: and be ready always to give an answer to every man that asketh you a reason of the hope that is in you with meekness and fear."

These verses show mission as teaching, presence, and humble explanation.

Think It Through

- Why does sharing belief often feel uncomfortable?
- How is representing different from pressuring?
- What does mission look like in everyday life?

WEEK 48 - WHAT IS HEAVEN?

The Big Question

Is heaven just a place people go when they die, or does Christianity mean something more by it?

Heaven is often imagined as clouds, angels, or an escape from life. Christianity presents a fuller picture that is tied to restoration, not disappearance.

The Christian Answer

Christianity teaches that heaven is life with God, not an abstract place.

Heaven is not mainly about location. It is about relationship. Christianity teaches that heaven means being fully restored to God's presence, free from sin, suffering, and death.

Heaven is also connected to the future of creation. Christianity does not teach that the goal is to leave the world behind forever. It teaches that God will renew what is broken. Heaven is part of that renewal, not a replacement for it.

This means heaven is not about boredom or floating existence. It is about life as it was meant to be. Joy, purpose, and relationship continue, without corruption or loss.

Because of this, heaven is not meant to make life now meaningless. It gives hope that brokenness is not permanent.

What the Bible Says (KJV)

John 14:2–3

"In my Father's house are many mansions: if it were not so, I would have told you. I go to prepare a place for you.

And if I go and prepare a place for you, I will come again, and receive you unto myself; that where I am, there ye may be also."

Revelation 21:3–4

"And I heard a great voice out of heaven saying, Behold, the tabernacle of God is with men, and he will dwell with them, and they shall be his people, and God himself shall be with them, and be their God.

And God shall wipe away all tears from their eyes; and there shall be no more death, neither sorrow, nor crying, neither shall there be any more pain: for the former things are passed away."

These verses describe heaven as God dwelling with people and removing suffering.

Think It Through

- Why do people often picture heaven as an escape rather than restoration?
- How does heaven being relational change how it is imagined?
- What kind of hope does renewal offer that escape does not?

WEEK 49 - WHAT IS HELL?

The Big Question

Why does Christianity talk about hell at all? Is it about punishment, fear, or something else?

Hell is one of the most difficult parts of Christian teaching. Many people reject it outright. Christianity includes it because it flows from how it understands God, freedom, and choice.

The Christian Answer

Christianity teaches that hell is separation from God, not a random punishment.

Hell is not described as God losing control or acting out of anger. It is the result of a final refusal of God. Christianity teaches that God does not force relationship. If someone rejects God, that rejection has real consequences.

Because God is the source of life, goodness, and joy, separation from God results in the absence of those things. Hell is not primarily about physical images. It is about the seriousness of choosing life apart from God.

Christianity also teaches that hell shows human choices matter. Actions and decisions are not meaningless. Freedom is real, and so are its outcomes.

This teaching is meant to be sober, not cruel. Christianity presents hell as a warning, not a threat, and as a reason to take truth seriously.

What the Bible Says (KJV)

Matthew 25:46

"And these shall go away into everlasting punishment: but the righteous into life eternal."

2 Thessalonians 1:8–9

"In flaming fire taking vengeance on them that know not God, and that obey not the gospel of our Lord Jesus Christ:

Who shall be punished with everlasting destruction from the presence of the Lord, and from the glory of his power."

These verses describe hell as separation from God and the outcome of rejecting him.

Think It Through

- Why does the idea of consequences make people uncomfortable?
- How does freedom require real outcomes to be meaningful?

WEEK 50 - WILL GOD JUDGE THE WORLD?

The Big Question

If God is loving, why would there be judgment at all?

Judgment often sounds harsh or unfair. Christianity includes it because it believes love, justice, and truth belong together.

The Christian Answer

Christianity teaches that judgment means God sets things right.

Judgment is not mainly about punishment. It is about justice. Christianity claims that evil, injustice, and wrongdoing matter, and that they will not be ignored forever. A world without judgment would be a world where nothing truly matters.

God's judgment also protects goodness. It says that harm, abuse, and cruelty are not acceptable and will not have the final word. Christianity teaches that God's judgment flows from his goodness, not against it.

At the same time, Christianity teaches that judgment is connected to mercy. Jesus' life, death, and resurrection are presented as God's way of offering forgiveness before judgment. Judgment is real, but it is not arbitrary or cruel.

Because of this, judgment is meant to be taken seriously without being used as a weapon. It points toward accountability and hope, not fear alone.

. . .

WHAT THE BIBLE Says (KJV)

Ecclesiastes 12:14

"For God shall bring every work into judgment, with every secret thing, whether it be good, or whether it be evil."

Romans 14:10–12

"For we shall all stand before the judgment seat of Christ.

For it is written, As I live, saith the Lord, every knee shall bow to me, and every tongue shall confess to God.

So then every one of us shall give account of himself to God."

These verses describe judgment as universal and connected to accountability.

THINK It Through

- Why would a world without judgment feel unfair?
- How can justice and love exist together?
- What does accountability say about the value of choices?

WEEK 51 - WHAT IS THE FUTURE CHRISTIANS HOPE FOR?

The Big Question

What exactly are Christians hoping for in the future, and why does it matter now?

Hope is often confused with wishful thinking. Christianity claims its hope is grounded in promises, not optimism.

The Christian Answer

Christianity teaches that the future is about restoration, not escape.

The Christian hope is not simply going to heaven when life ends. It is the promise that God will fully restore what sin and death have broken. This includes people, relationships, and creation itself.

Christianity teaches that Jesus will return to complete this restoration. Evil will be defeated, justice will be established, and life will be renewed. The future is not uncertain or meaningless. It is moving toward a purpose.

This hope also shapes life now. Because the future is secure, Christians are called to live with faithfulness, courage, and patience in the present. Hope gives direction, not passivity.

Christian hope is not denial of pain. It is confidence that pain is not permanent.

. . .

What the Bible Says (KJV)

Revelation 21:5

"And he that sat upon the throne said, Behold, I make all things new. And he said unto me, Write: for these words are true and faithful."

1 Corinthians 15:58

"Therefore, my beloved brethren, be ye stedfast, unmoveable, always abounding in the work of the Lord, forasmuch as ye know that your labour is not in vain in the Lord."

These verses describe a future of renewal that gives meaning to present faithfulness.

Think It Through

- How is hope different from wishing things would turn out well?
- Why does belief about the future affect how people live now?
- What does restoration offer that escape does not?

WEEK 52 - WHAT DOES IT ALL MEAN?

The Big Question

After learning all of this, what is someone actually supposed to do with it?

It is easy to treat beliefs as information. Christianity claims they are meant to shape real life, not just understanding.

The Christian Answer

Christianity teaches that truth calls for response.

Knowing Christian beliefs is not the end goal. The goal is trust, alignment, and lived faith. Christianity claims that what someone believes about God, humanity, sin, and salvation will inevitably shape how they live.

Living this out does not mean having everything figured out. It means choosing direction. Following Jesus involves ongoing learning, repentance, trust, and growth. The Christian life is not about reaching a final level. It is about walking forward.

Christianity also teaches that faith is lived in ordinary life. School, friendships, work, choices, and struggles all become places where belief shows up. There is no separate category for "spiritual life" that exists apart from daily life.

This final week is not a conclusion so much as a beginning. Christianity claims that understanding leads to commitment, and commitment leads to a transformed way of living.

What the Bible Says (KJV)

James 1:22

"But be ye doers of the word, and not hearers only, deceiving your own selves."

Matthew 7:24

"Therefore whosoever heareth these sayings of mine, and doeth them, I will liken him unto a wise man, which built his house upon a rock."

These verses connect understanding with action and stability.

Think It Through

- Why is it easier to learn ideas than to live them out?
- What does direction look like when perfection is not the goal?
- How might belief quietly shape everyday choices?

www.ingramcontent.com/pod-product-compliance
Lightning Source LLC
LaVergne TN
LVHW010933110826
845149LV00013B/2578

* 9 7 9 8 9 9 8 7 2 4 2 8 2 *